D1275528

ECONOMY IN ACTION!

ECONOMIC SYSTEMS

Tamara L. Britton
ABDO Publishing Company

visit us at
www.abdopublishing.com

Printed in the United States of America, North Mankato, Minnesota.
052012
092012

 PRINTED ON RECYCLED PAPER

Cover Photo: Alamy
Interior Photos: Alamy pp. 19, 21, 23; AP Images pp. 9, 10, 13, 14–15, 17, 24–25;
    Corbis pp. 5, 12; iStockphoto pp. 1, 7, 27; Library of Congress p. 8

Editors: Megan M. Gunderson, Stephanie Hedlund
Art Direction: Neil Klinepier

Library of Congress Cataloging-in-Publication Data

Britton, Tamara L., 1963-
 Economic systems / Tamara L. Britton.
    p. cm. -- (Economy in action!)
 ISBN 978-1-61783-486-8
 1. Economics. 2. Economic policy. I. Title.
 HB171.B6497 2013
 330.1--dc23
                                    2012016681

Contents

What Is an Economy?

We've been hearing about the economy a lot lately. Businesses are selling fewer products. Millions of people do not have jobs. But what does it all mean?

Well, it starts with needs and wants. We need food, clothing, and shelter. We want tablet computers, video games, and skinny jeans.

Some needs become wants. We need food, but want French fries. We need clothing, but want it from Hollister. We need shelter, but want a house with a swimming pool.

As you can see, our needs and wants are unlimited. But we have limited **resources**. We have a set amount of money. The earth has only so much fresh air, oil, clean water, and space. We can't have everything!

So, societies must decide what products to produce with their available resources. They must decide who produces them and how they are **distributed**. The system within which these decisions are made and carried out is the economy.

When you shop, are you satisfying needs or wants?

How Does an Economy Work?

Businesses produce goods and services. To do this, they buy **resources**. Businesses demand labor and **capital**. People **supply** labor with their time and capital with their money. People demand goods and services to satisfy their needs and wants. All these actions happen in markets.

There are two economic forces at work in these actions. They are supply and demand. These affect prices for resources, capital, labor, goods, and services. Prices rise when demand exceeds supply. Prices lower if supply overtakes demand.

Competition is another economic force. Many businesses can produce the same product. People shopping for the product will decide what to buy, where to buy it, and how much they will pay. So, competition also sets prices.

When businesses are making money, the economy grows. This is the top of the **business cycle**.

In the United States, the nation is at full employment if just four percent of workers aged 16 and older are unemployed.

Economic Theories

Okay, now you know what an economy is. You also know how it works. There's a lot going on! But how can an economy best satisfy everyone? Those who study this are called economists. Some have ideas that they believe would create the best economy.

One of the first was Adam Smith. In 1776, he wrote *The Wealth of Nations*.

Adam Smith is known as the founder of modern economics.

FUN FACT

The full title of Smith's book is An Inquiry into the Nature and Causes of the Wealth of Nations.

Smith argued that markets be allowed to work free of interference. He believed this would be the best system.

But not everyone thought free markets were best. In 1848, Karl Marx wrote *Manifesto of the Communist Party*. He argued that free market economies create an imbalance.

The phrase "From each according to his ability, to each according to his needs" was popularized by Karl Marx.

FUN FACT

Marx's Manifesto of the Communist Party *is known as* The Communist Manifesto.

Keynes's ideas are known as Keynesian economics.

People who own the means of production, such as farms and factories, control most of the wealth. Marx believed this would cause such a free market system to fail.

In 1936, John Maynard Keynes wrote *The General Theory of Employment, **Interest**, and Money*. His theory also contrasted with Smith's. Keynes believed a healthy economy depended on demand. So, in a downturn, government should borrow and spend money to influence demand. Money earned in the following growth period could repay the debt.

GOVERNMENTS AND ECONOMIES

Don't confuse governments and economic systems. They are not the same! For example, the United States and Mexico are federal republics with free market economies. Venezuela is a federal republic with a managed economy.

Friedrich Hayek disagreed. He believed that economies were too **complex** for anyone to understand. In his 1944 book *The Road to Serfdom*, Hayek said governments should not try to manage their economies.

These are wide-ranging opinions! How do we determine what really works best? Nations test these ideas in their economic systems.

Hayek was part of the Austrian School of Economics. Austrian economists believe interference by governments and central banks does not help economies and can actually damage them.

There are three basic types of economic systems. Each answers three key questions. How does a society use its **resources** to produce goods and services? How does it effectively **allocate** and **distribute** them? And, is it the best way to satisfy everyone's needs and wants? Let's take a look!

13

Traditional Economies

The first economies were traditional systems. Families produced what they needed. Men and women had different roles. Each was important in the survival of the family or group.

Today, traditional economies are rare. The Yanomami Indians live in an isolated part of South America. They have a traditional economy.

Yanomami families live in large villages. A village is made of a large, circular shelter.

It is built by the families who will live in it. Within the shelter, each family has its own space.

The families survive by farming, hunting, and gathering. Each family has its own garden. The men clear the fields. Both men and women do the planting. The women mostly do the weeding and harvesting. Hunting is a job for men only.

All Yanomami participate in foraging and gathering. Women cook and care for the children. In traditional economies, families provide for themselves. Otherwise, they cannot satisfy their needs and wants.

Today, Venezuela and Brazil's expanding populations crowd the Yanomami's homelands. But, contact with these economies allows the Yanomami to have goods they cannot produce themselves such this boy's mirror.

Free Market Economies

As you can see, traditional economies can work in some societies. But in **complex** societies, each family cannot produce everything it needs and wants.

In free market systems, land, factories, and **resources** are privately owned. So, private decision makers determine how resources are used.

Businesses buy resources and labor to produce goods and services. Heads of businesses decide what goods and services will be produced. They also decide how they will be **distributed**.

In the marketplace, products compete against each other for people's money. Prices are set by **supply** and demand.

In a free market, people can start their own businesses. Or, they can choose to work at businesses that offer the best jobs. The more they work, the more money they can make. This allows them to build more wealth.

FUN FACT

Free market economies are also called capitalist or laissez-faire economies. Laissez-faire is a French term. It means "allow to do."

A free market may seem like a free-for-all! But, governments do impose some rules. For example, they manage hiring policies, building codes, and **minimum** wages. But it is individuals seeking better living conditions and more money who make a free market economy work.

The United States has a free market economy. In 2011, 543,000 people each month started their own businesses. This 10-year-old boy owns his own ice cream stand in New Hampshire.

Managed Economies

The free market economy rewards **initiative**, ambition, and **ingenuity**. However, not everyone has these qualities. So, some people can achieve less economic success than others.

In addition, not everyone has access to markets. And, some people cannot sell their labor to buy goods and services. So, they have a lower **standard of living**.

Marx thought if an economy were managed more closely, society's wealth would be **distributed** more equally. Then, there would not be such a big gap between rich and poor.

In a managed economy, the government planners make most major economic decisions. The public or the state owns all means of production. These can be land, timber, factories, farms, and mines.

FUN FACT

Managed economies are also called centrally-planned or command economies.

Planners tell businesses what to produce, who to hire, and how much to pay employees. They decide how goods and services are **distributed**. They also decide how much goods and services cost. This way, the government manages society's wealth.

However, this system limits personal freedoms. As a result, people who live within managed economies may not work hard if their efforts offer no chance to advance. If the reward for working hard is not more money, better food, or other goods, people who do work may not do so for long.

Cuba has a managed economy. The government determines how much food is distributed to each citizen. Ration books keep track of each person's share.

Mixed Economies

So what to do? The traditional economy does not fit **complex** societies. Free market economies offer individual freedom. But, they do not do a good job **distributing** wealth. Managed economies control wealth distribution. But, they limit freedom and can lower **initiative**.

Would a compromise be a good solution? What if the government and market could each play a part? This theory became the mixed economy.

In a mixed economy, markets decide how **resources** are used and what goods and services are produced. They decide how they are distributed and who receives them in some industries. The government decides how these questions will be answered in other industries.

For example, a person is free to start a restaurant. She can hire whomever she wants. She can pay her employees a market wage. She can buy meats and vegetables in the open market and sell her food at a competitive price.

France has a mixed economy. One of the industries the government controls is transportation. The TGV is the nation's high-speed train service.

However, the government regulates the energy company. It decides what **resources** the company is able to use, and how it should use them. It also decides how much the company can charge the people for its energy.

In a mixed economy, people have the freedom to start businesses. They can create their own success. However, government regulation keeps wealth from concentrating in certain areas.

What If the Economy Isn't Working?

You learned earlier that when an economy grows, businesses and people make money. They spend money to satisfy their needs and wants. This is called a boom.

But sometimes the economy contracts. Businesses aren't selling their goods and services. They have less money to spend on labor. So, people lose their jobs. They can't earn money to spend. This is called a bust.

A slow economy can cause much suffering. When businesses close, workers can be **unemployed** for months. If an economy does not recover, it can slip into a **recession**. Or worse, it can face a **depression**.

All economies are subject to booms and busts in the **business cycle**. Hayek suggested that a struggling economy would return to **equilibrium** if left alone. But how long should the economy be left to linger? Should steps be taken to get it working again? If so, what should be done?

During periods of high unemployment, many people can't buy enough food. In 2010, 16 million American children were food insecure. At food banks, thousands of volunteers pack food boxes to meet these needs.

Keynes argued that **stimulating** demand would spark the economy. There are many ways governments do this. Central banks can lower **interest** rates. This makes borrowing money less expensive. So, people and businesses can get loans.

After the **Great Recession** began, President George W. Bush signed the Troubled **Asset** Relief Program in 2008. In this program, the federal government bought assets from banks. Then, banks had more money to lend.

Governments can also provide jobs. To this end,

President Barack Obama signed the American Recovery and Reinvestment Act (ARRA) in 2009. Officials estimated that the act would create 3.5 million jobs by the end of 2010.

Governments can also lower tax rates. In 2010, President Obama lowered the payroll tax rate. This gave workers more money in their paychecks. With more money to spend, they could buy more goods and services.

The ARRA included funding for electric vehicles. In Detroit, Michigan, 1,350 employees work to build Chevrolet Volts.

Seeking the Best for All

Now you understand the economy and basic economic systems. So, what do you think? Which system is best? Keep in mind that different nations have different **resources**. And different people have different **cultures** and **priorities**.

But everyone wants nutritious food, clean water, protective clothing, and safe shelter. And, nobody wants to see others suffer from an economic contraction.

So, is the best system the managed economy that requires people to earn, work, spend, and give what government planners decide? Or is it the free market system that lets people do what they want? Is it the mixed economy that tries to do both?

Perhaps no economic system will work best for every society. But we will keep trying to find the best way to adequately provide for everyone!

There are more than 7 billion people on Earth! We must work together to satisfy our needs and wants.

MANAGING RESOURCES

Which resources are needed to produce which goods and services?

RESOURCES

a) gold   b) silver   c) timber   d) corn   e) petroleum

GOODS AND SERVICES

7. gasoline

10. dentistry

9. breakfast cereal

3. ethanol

6. bracelets

8. animal feed

4. burn medicine

11. baseball bats

5. lumber

1. batteries

12. fertilizer

2. paper

Answer Key:
a) 6, 10 b) 1, 4, 6, 10 c) 2, 5, 11 d) 3, 8, 9 e) 7, 12

Imagine you are a government planner in a managed economy. Which goods and services would you produce with these resources? Ask a friend which he or she would choose. Were the choices different? Could you make these choices well enough to provide for an entire nation's needs and wants?

WANTS vs. NEEDS

Which is a want and which is a need? It is not always easy to tell, is it? If you were wealthy, would it change your answers? What if you had no money?

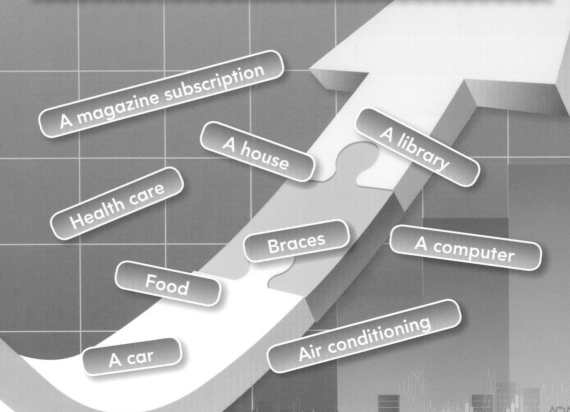

A magazine subscription

A house

A library

Health care

Braces

A computer

Food

A car

Air conditioning

Glossary

allocate - to divide and give out something for a special reason or to particular people or companies.

asset - something of value owned by a person, a business, or a government.

business cycle - changing levels of economic activity over time. The five stages of the business cycle are growth, peak, contraction, trough, and recovery.

capital - the factories and equipment owned by a business and used to make money.

complex - having many parts, details, ideas, or functions.

culture - the customs, arts, and tools of a nation or people at a certain time.

depression - a period of economic trouble when there is little buying or selling and many people are out of work.

distribute - to give out or deliver something to each individual in a group.

equilibrium - a state in which opposing forces are balanced.

Great Recession - beginning in 2007, a period of time when business activity slowed.

ingenuity - the skill or cleverness to solve problems, start businesses, or invent things.

initiative - the power or opportunity to do something before others do.

interest - money paid for the use or borrowing of money.

minimum - the least amount possible.

priority - the condition of coming before others, as in order or importance.

recession - a period of time when business activity slows.

resources - something that can be used to increase wealth.

standard of living - the amount of wealth, comfort, and possessions that a person or group has.

stimulate - to excite to activity or growth or to greater activity.

supply - the amount of something available for sale.

unemployment - the state of being out of work. Someone who is out of work is unemployed.

Web Sites

To learn more about the economy in action, visit ABDO Publishing Company online. Web sites about economic systems are featured on our Book Links page. These links are routinely monitored and updated to provide the most current information available.

www.abdopublishing.com

Index